Downers Grove Public Library
1050 Curtiss St.
Downers Grove, IL 60515

2|09-64

Pebble® Plus

Exploring the Galaxy
Mercury

by Thomas K. Adamson

Consulting Editor: Gail Saunders-Smith, PhD

Consultant: James Gerard
Aerospace Education Specialist, NASA
Kennedy Space Center, Florida

Capstone press®
Mankato, Minnesota

Pebble Plus is published by Capstone Press,
151 Good Counsel Drive, P.O. Box 669, Mankato, Minnesota 56002.
www.capstonepress.com

1 2 3 4 5 6 12 11 10 09 08 07

Library of Congress Cataloging-in-Publication Data
Adamson, Thomas K., 1970–
     Mercury / by Thomas K. Adamson.—Rev. and updated.
     p. cm.—(Pebble plus. Exploring the galaxy)
     Includes bibliographical references and index.
     ISBN-13: 978-1-4296-0735-3 (hardcover)
     ISBN-10: 1-4296-0735-1 (hardcover)
     1. Mercury (Planet)—Juvenile literature. I. Title. II. Series.
QB611.A33 2008
523.41—dc22   2007004453

Summary: Simple text and photographs describe the planet Mercury.

Editorial Credits
Mari C. Schuh, editor; Kia Adams, designer; Alta Schaffer, photo researcher

Photo Credits
Digital Vision, 5 (Venus)
NASA, 13, 15; JPL, 5 (Jupiter); JPL/Caltech, 5 (Uranus), 11, 17
PhotoDisc Inc., cover, 4 (Neptune); 5 (Mars, Mercury, Earth, Sun, Saturn); 9 (both), 19; Stock Trek, 1; PhotoDisc Imaging, 7
Photo Researchers/Frank Zullo, 21

Note to Parents and Teachers

The Exploring the Galaxy set supports national science standards related to earth science. This book
describes and illustrates the planet Mercury. The photographs support early readers in understanding the
text. The repetition of words and phrases helps early readers learn new words. This book also introduces
early readers to subject-specific vocabulary words, which are defined in the Glossary section. Early readers
may need assistance to read some words and to use the Table of Contents, Glossary, Read More, Internet Sites,
and Index sections of the book.

Table of Contents

Mercury

Mercury is the closest planet

to the Sun.

Mercury moves around

the Sun faster than

any other planet.

The Solar System

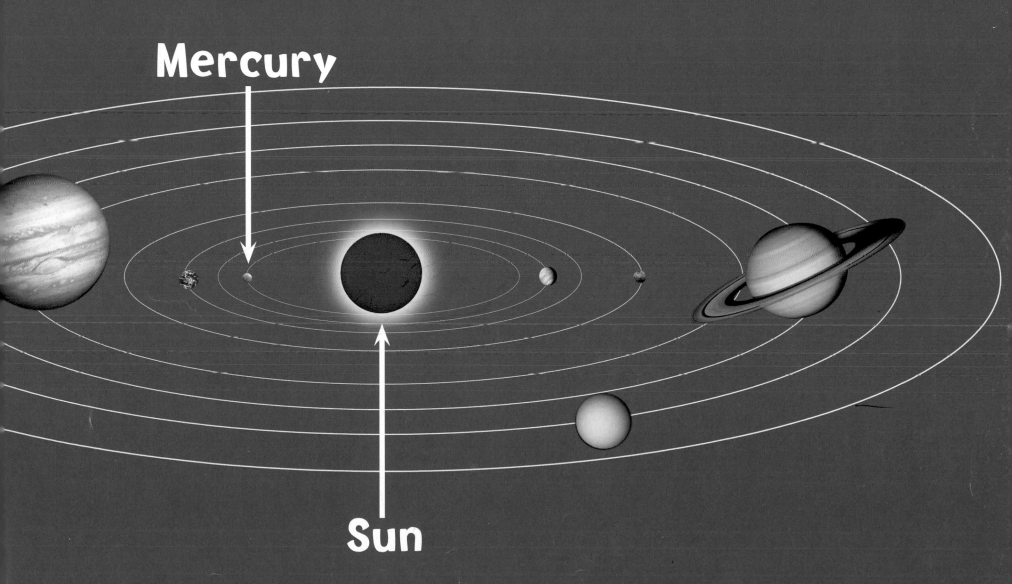

Mercury

Sun

Mercury can be colder than
a freezer at night.
Mercury can be hotter than
an oven during the day.

7

Mercury's Size

Mercury is the second smallest planet. Earth is three times wider than Mercury.

Earth

Mercury

9

Mercury's Surface

Mercury is a rocky planet.

The surface of Mercury

looks like Earth's moon.

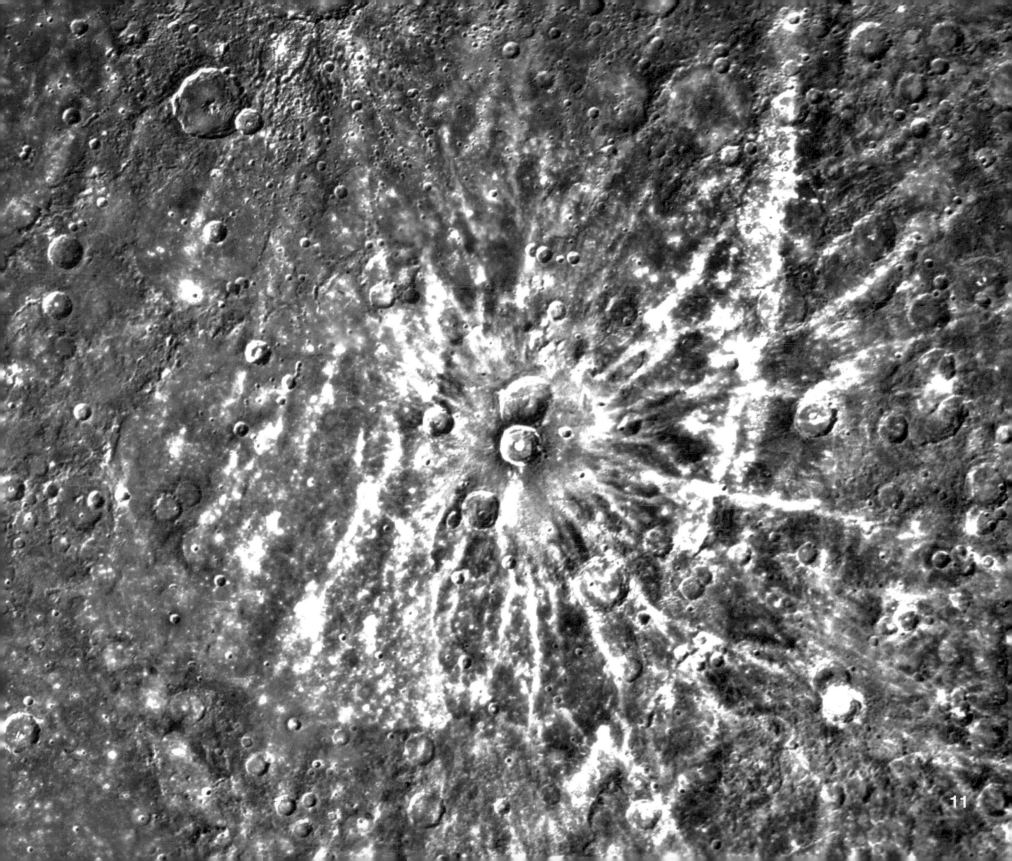

11

Mercury's surface looks gray.

Dust covers the surface.

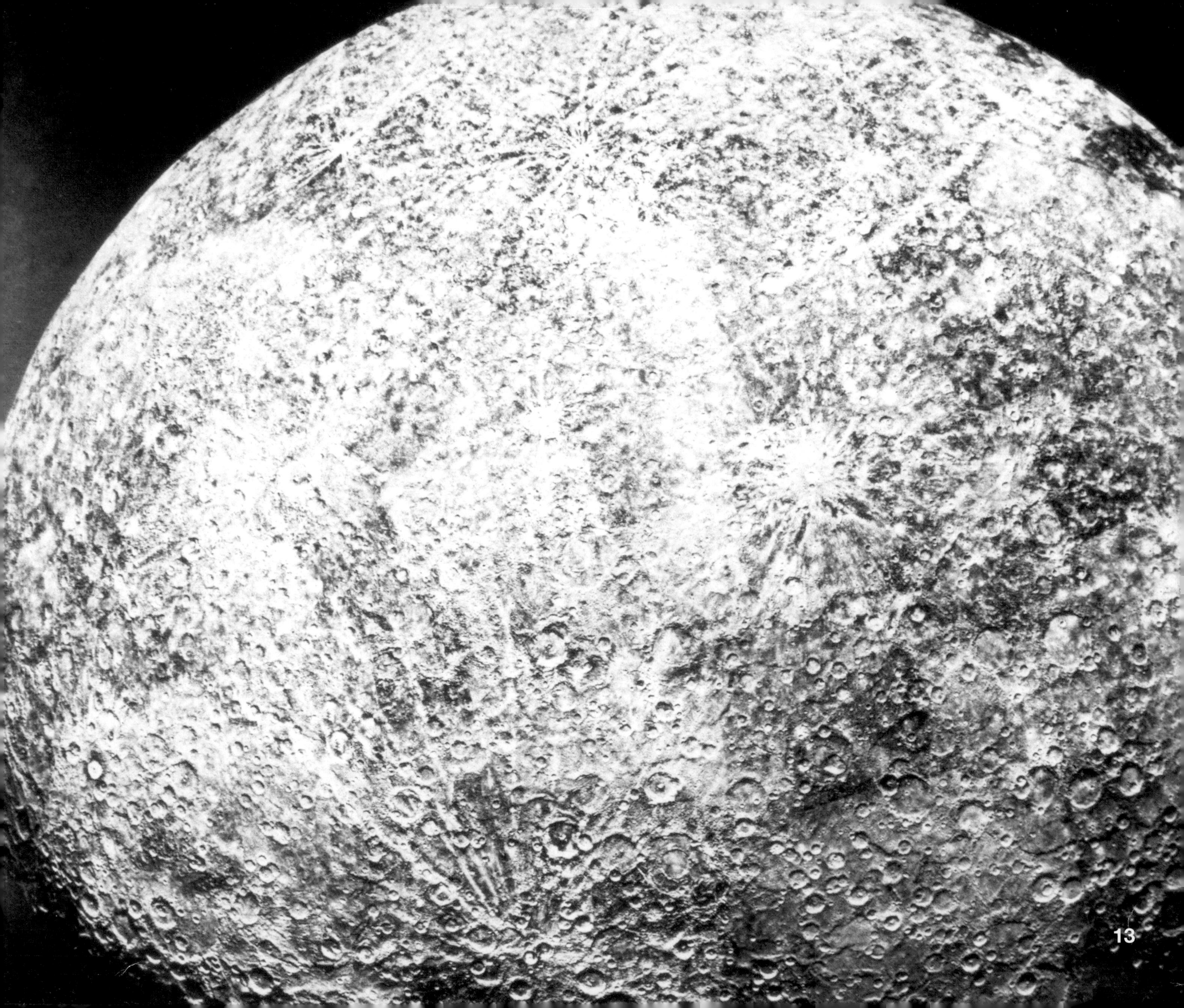

Craters cover

Mercury's surface.

Large rocks called asteroids

made these holes.

15

Craters near the planet's

poles have ice.

Sunlight cannot shine

on the ice to melt it.

17

People and Mercury

Mercury does not have

air or water.

People and animals

could not live on Mercury.

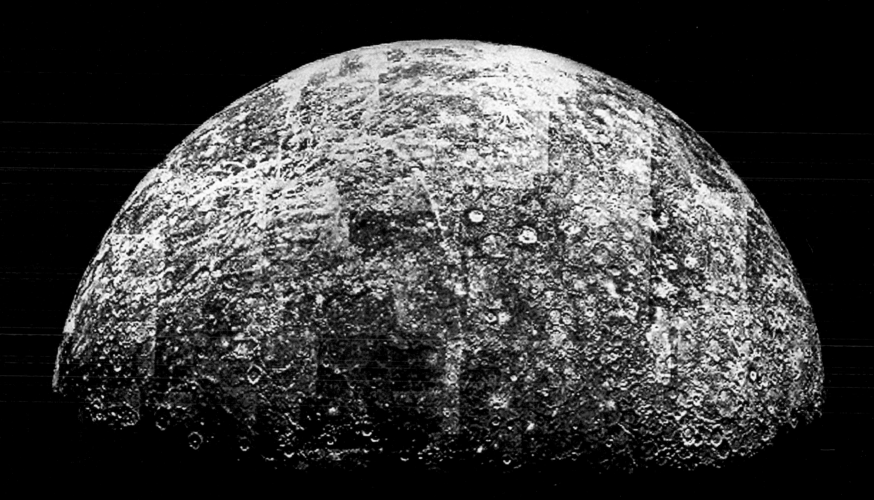

People can sometimes
see Mercury from Earth.
Mercury looks like a dim star.

Mercury ⟶ ·

Glossary

asteroid—a large space rock that moves around the Sun

crater—a large bowl-shaped hole in the ground

dim—somewhat dark; dim stars are not very bright.

moon—an object that moves around a planet; Earth has one moon; Mercury does not have any moons.

planet—a large object that moves around the Sun; Mercury is the closest planet to the Sun; there are eight planets in the solar system.

pole—the top or bottom part of a planet

star—a large ball of burning gases in space; the Sun is a star.

Sun—the star that the planets move around; the Sun provides light and heat for the planets.

Read More

Bredeson, Carmen. *What Is the Solar System?* I Like Space! Berkeley Heights, N.J.: Enslow, 2008.

Richardson, Adele. *Mercury*. First Facts: The Solar System. Mankato, Minn.: Capstone Press, 2008.

Wimmer, Teresa. *Mercury*. My First Look at Planets. Mankato, Minn.: Creative Education, 2007.

Internet Sites

FactHound offers a safe, fun way to find Internet sites related to this book. All of the sites on FactHound have been researched by our staff.

Here's how:

1. Visit *www.facthound.com*

2. Choose your grade level.

3. Type in this book ID **1429607351** for age-appropriate sites. You may also browse subjects by clicking on letters, or by clicking on pictures and words.

4. Click on the **Fetch It** button.

FactHound will fetch the best sites for you!

Index

Word Count: 126
Grade: 1
Early-Intervention Level: 15